10,000-HOUR
PRACTICE LOG & JOURNAL

THE PERFECT TOOL FOR
TRACKING YOUR JOURNEY
TOWARD MASTERY

CREATED BY MARK POWERS
POWERSPERCUSSION.COM

The 10,000-hour rule:

Many experts agree that becoming a "master" in any particular field or pursuit requires one to put in a minimum of 10,000 hours of deliberate practice in that area. It's certainly true that it takes more than *only* time (e.g. proper technique; correct decisions about what specifically to be working on; etc.), but logging that much focused time will most definitely be beneficial to anyone striving to increase their abilities and realize their dreams.

If you're truly dead serious about that instrument you want to play professionally, or that art career you want, isn't it time to step up your game, start tracking those hours, and do the work?

This practice log/journal is the perfect tool for that purpose. You'll be guided along page-by-page, prompted to enter details about each practice session, including the date, time and duration; your mood and/or energy level going into the session; goals for that specific practice stretch; and what went well/poorly. There will also be room to write additional notes about that particular session, or perhaps thoughts for the next one.

The following page is an example of what a completed log entry might look like – this one filled out by a student of percussion.

Date & time: June 3, 2015   3:30pm
Duration: 1.5 hours

Mood/energy: Tired (stayed up too late)

Goals/plan:

- hands: Syncopation pages 40&41, alternated 8th-note triplets + flams
- bass drum: New Breed melody III-B with system 4
- push half-time shuffle tempo

* Sync. finally feels good at 80 bpm
* snare drum ghost notes are quieter on half-time shuffle!!

* right foot gets tense when playing doubles

Notes & comments:

- repeat New Breed (III-B) next time, but slow down . . . and RELAX!

- try Syncopation at 82-86 bpm

- shuffle: add bass drum variations

If used daily, this log will help you record approximately three months' worth of practices. Near the back of the book, you'll find graphs that you can use to track your gradual progress toward that 10,000-hour milestone.

Throughout these pages, you'll also find occasional journal pages, which will cue you to reflect and write your thoughts on a variety of matters related to the hard work you're undergoing.

Space will be reserved for you to list long-term goals, for your reference while working through this log, and for transferring into future logs that you move into. You should refer to this list as you plan goals and exercises for your individual practice sessions.

After completely filling this log, enter your date range and total hour information in the spots designated for each on the front/back covers, and do the accompanying math to find your total accumulated hours. As you work through additional logs, this will give you a quick reference of what you've accomplished and how the progress you're making toward that magical 10,000 hours!

**A note to private instructors
and classroom teachers:**

Regardless of whether or not you set 10,000 hours as an ultimate goal for your students, this log can be an extremely useful tool for tracking their practice time.

In the "goals/plan" sections, you can help a student to lay out what he/she should be focusing on for a given session. Or utilize several pages and help organize their entire upcoming week of practice times.

Reviewing recent log entries during a lesson can aid in helping the student to see how/where their time is being used best; what areas are being neglected; etc.

If you insist on "X" number of practice hours each week, you might also consider requiring a parent's signature on each page, verifying that session time was logged.

My long-term goals:

- _____
- _____
- _____
- _____
- _____
- _____
- _____
- _____
- _____
- _____
- _____
- _____
- _____
- _____
- _____
- _____

In regards to your area of interest/pursuit, what do you see (right now) as your two biggest weaknesses?

And your two biggest strengths?

Date & time:
Duration:

Mood/energy:

Goals/plan:

Notes & comments:

"Practice does not make perfect; it makes permanent." ~ Alexander Libermann

Date & time:
Duration:

Mood/energy:

Goals/plan:

Notes & comments:

"The best way for a student to get out of difficulty is to go through it." ~ Aristotle

Date & time:
Duration:

Mood/energy:

Goals/plan:

Notes & comments:

"Success is the sum of small efforts, repeated day in and day out." ~ *Robert Collier*

Date & time:
Duration:

Mood/energy:

Goals/plan:

Notes & comments:

Date & time:
Duration:

Mood/energy:

Goals/plan:

Notes & comments:

"Opportunities don't happen. You create them." ~ Chris Grosser

Date & time:
Duration:

Mood/energy:

Goals/plan:

Notes & comments:

"All progress takes place outside the comfort zone." ~ Michael John Bobak

Date & time:
Duration:

Mood/energy:

Goals/plan:

Notes & comments:

"The most valuable practice aid is patience." ~ Howard Snell

Name three people who are current creative influences.

And one thing that each of them inspires you to do, learn or change.

Date & time:
Duration:

Mood/energy:

Goals/plan:

Notes & comments:

"If you want to make a permanent change, stop focusing on the size of your problems and start focusing on the size of you!" ~ T. Harv Eker

Date & time:
Duration:

Mood/energy:

Goals/plan:

Notes & comments:

"To follow, without halt, one aim: There's the secret of success." ~ Anna Pavlova

Date & time:
Duration:

Mood/energy:

Goals/plan:

Notes & comments:

"It is important to practice at the speed of no mistakes." ~ *Lucinda Mackworth-Young*

Date & time:
Duration:

Mood/energy:

Goals/plan:

+

−

Notes & comments:

Date & time:
Duration:

Mood/energy:

Goals/plan:

Notes & comments:

Date & time:
Duration:

Mood/energy:

Goals/plan:

Notes & comments:

"The difference between knowledge and skill is practice." ~ *Holly Marie Simmers*

Date & time:
Duration:

Mood/energy:

Goals/plan:

Notes & comments:

"If I don't practice the way I should, then I won't play the way that I know I can." ~ Ivan Lendl

List two past accomplishments you've made.

Then, for each, list something that, if/when reached, you would see as growth and a further success beyond that initial accomplishment.

Date & time:
Duration:

Mood/energy:

Goals/plan:

Notes & comments:

Date & time:
Duration:

Mood/energy:

Goals/plan:

Notes & comments:

Date & time:
Duration:

Mood/energy:

Goals/plan:

Notes & comments:

"None of us really pushes hard enough." ~ *Fran Tarkenton*

Date & time:
Duration:

Mood/energy:

Goals/plan:

+

−

Notes & comments:

"Practice, which some regard as a chore, should be approached as just about the most pleasant recreation ever devised." ~ Babe Didrikson Zaharias

Date & time:
Duration:

Mood/energy:

Goals/plan:

Notes & comments:

"I never wanted to leave the court until I got things exactly correct.
My dream was to become a pro." ~ Larry Bird

Date & time:
Duration:

Mood/energy:

Goals/plan:

Notes & comments:

Date & time:
Duration:

Mood/energy:

Goals/plan:

Notes & comments:

"Determination, effort, and practice are rewarded with success."
~ Mary Lydon Simonsen

Why do you want to become a master at this?

Date & time:
Duration:

Mood/energy:

Goals/plan:

Notes & comments:

"You go on. You set one foot in front of the other, and if a thin voice cries out, somewhere behind you, you pretend not to hear, and keep going."
~ *Geraldine Brooks*

Date & time:
Duration:

Mood/energy:

Goals/plan:

Notes & comments:

Date & time:
Duration:

Mood/energy:

Goals/plan:

Notes & comments:

Date & time:
Duration:

Mood/energy:

Goals/plan:

Notes & comments:

Date & time:
Duration:

Mood/energy:

Goals/plan:

Notes & comments:

"A river cuts through rock, not because of its power, but because of its persistence." ~ Jim Watkins

Date & time:
Duration:

Mood/energy:

Goals/plan:

Notes & comments:

"It does not matter how slowly you go as long as you do not stop." ~ Confucius

Date & time:
Duration:

Mood/energy:

Goals/plan:

Notes & comments:

"For success, attitude is equally as important as ability." ~ Harry F. Banks

What do you feel have been two areas of growth and improvement so far as you've worked through the past days, hours and pages of this practice log?

Date & time:
Duration:

Mood/energy:

Goals/plan:

Notes & comments:

Date & time:
Duration:

Mood/energy:

Goals/plan:

+

−

Notes & comments:

Date & time:
Duration:

Mood/energy:

Goals/plan:

Notes & comments:

"Do it badly; do it slowly; do it fearfully;
do it any way you have to, but do it." ~ Steve Chandler

Date & time:
Duration:

Mood/energy:

Goals/plan:

Notes & comments:

Date & time:
Duration:

Mood/energy:

Goals/plan:

+

−

Notes & comments:

"Judge your success by what you had to give up in order to get it." ~ Dalai Lama

Date & time:
Duration:

Mood/energy:

Goals/plan:

Notes & comments:

"Energy and persistence conquer all things." ~ Benjamin Franklin

Date & time:
Duration:

Mood/energy:

Goals/plan:

$+$

$-$

Notes & comments:

"Tomorrow's victory is today's practice." ~ *Chris Bradford*

What stops you from practicing more than you currently do?

Date & time:
Duration:

Mood/energy:

Goals/plan:

Notes & comments:

"Champions keep playing until they get it right." ~ Billy Jean King

Date & time:
Duration:

Mood/energy:

Goals/plan:

Notes & comments:

"It always seems impossible until it is done." ~ Nelson Mandela

Date & time:
Duration:

Mood/energy:

Goals/plan:

+

−

Notes & comments:

Date & time:
Duration:

Mood/energy:

Goals/plan:

Notes & comments:

"Without practice, nothing can be achieved." ~ Swami Satchidananda

Date & time:
Duration:

Mood/energy:

Goals/plan:

Notes & comments:

"Successful people keep moving. They make mistakes,
but they don't quit." ~ Conrad Hilton

Date & time:
Duration:

Mood/energy:

Goals/plan:

Notes & comments:

Date & time:
Duration:

Mood/energy:

Goals/plan:

+

−

Notes & comments:

*"Consider the postage stamp: Its usefulness consists in
he ability to stick to one thing till it gets there." ~ Josh Billings*

Name four life achievements that you truly hope to reach. Feel free to think as big and crazy as you want!

Date & time:
Duration:

Mood/energy:

Goals/plan:

Notes & comments:

*"Good things come to those who work their asses off
and never give up." (author unknown)*

Date & time:
Duration:

Mood/energy:

Goals/plan:

Notes & comments:

Date & time:
Duration:

Mood/energy:

Goals/plan:

Notes & comments:

"Practice does not make perfect;
perfect practice makes perfect." ~ Vince Lombardi

Date & time:
Duration:

Mood/energy:

Goals/plan:

Notes & comments:

"The difference between try and triumph is just a little umph!" ~ Marvin Phillips

Date & time:
Duration:

Mood/energy:

Goals/plan:

Notes & comments:

Date & time:
Duration:

Mood/energy:

Goals/plan:

Notes & comments:

Date & time:
Duration:

Mood/energy:

Goals/plan:

Notes & comments:

What habit(s) is/are holding you back from going further faster?

Date & time:
Duration:

Mood/energy:

Goals/plan:

Notes & comments:

Date & time:
Duration:

Mood/energy:

Goals/plan:

Notes & comments:

Date & time:
Duration:

Mood/energy:

Goals/plan:

Notes & comments:

Date & time:
Duration:

Mood/energy:

Goals/plan:

Notes & comments:

Date & time:
Duration:

Mood/energy:

Goals/plan:

Notes & comments:

"The successful warrior is the average man, with laser-like focus." ~ Bruce Lee

Date & time:
Duration:

Mood/energy:

Goals/plan:

Notes & comments:

Date & time:
Duration:

Mood/energy:

Goals/plan:

Notes & comments:

*"Character is what emerges from all the little things
you were too busy to do yesterday, but did anyway." ~ Mignon McLaughlin*

For a successful career in this, what are things that you feel you may need to sacrifice (now and/or in the future)?

Date & time:
Duration:

Mood/energy:

Goals/plan:

Notes & comments:

Date & time:
Duration:

Mood/energy:

Goals/plan:

Notes & comments:

Date & time:
Duration:

Mood/energy:

Goals/plan:

Notes & comments:

Date & time:
Duration:

Mood/energy:

Goals/plan:

Notes & comments:

"Though the barriers of life seem formidable, we find
when we challenge them that they have no will." ~ Robert Brault

Date & time:
Duration:

Mood/energy:

Goals/plan:

Notes & comments:

"Those at the top of the mountain didn't fall there." (author unknown)

Date & time:
Duration:

Mood/energy:

Goals/plan:

Notes & comments:

Date & time:
Duration:

Mood/energy:

Goals/plan:

Notes & comments:

"The difference between a successful person and others is not a lack of strength, not a lack of knowledge, but rather a lack of will." ~ Vince Lombardi

What motivates you more than anything else?

Date & time:
Duration:

Mood/energy:

Goals/plan:

Notes & comments:

"The elevator to success is not running; you must climb the stairs." ~ Zig Ziglar

Date & time:
Duration:

Mood/energy:

Goals/plan:

Notes & comments:

Date & time:
Duration:

Mood/energy:

Goals/plan:

Notes & comments:

Date & time:
Duration:

Mood/energy:

Goals/plan:

Notes & comments:

Date & time:
Duration:

Mood/energy:

Goals/plan:

Notes & comments:

Date & time:
Duration:

Mood/energy:

Goals/plan:

Notes & comments:

Date & time:
Duration:

Mood/energy:

Goals/plan:

+

−

Notes & comments:

"Do not be embarrassed by your failures, learn from them and start again."
~ Richard Branson

You've been reading plenty of success, practice and motivation quotes on these pages.

Make up your own below.

Date & time:
Duration:

Mood/energy:

Goals/plan:

+

−

Notes & comments:

"You've got to get up every morning with determination
if you're going to go to bed with satisfaction." ~ George Lorimer

Date & time:
Duration:

Mood/energy:

Goals/plan:

Notes & comments:

"All roads that lead to success have to pass through Hard Work Boulevard at some point." ~ Eric Thomas

Date & time:
Duration:

Mood/energy:

Goals/plan:

Notes & comments:

"If you want to make an easy job seem mighty hard,
just keep putting off doing it." ~ Olin Miller

Date & time:
Duration:

Mood/energy:

Goals/plan:

Notes & comments:

Date & time:
Duration:

Mood/energy:

Goals/plan:

Notes & comments:

Date & time:
Duration:

Mood/energy:

Goals/plan:

Notes & comments:

Date & time:
Duration:

Mood/energy:

Goals/plan:

Notes & comments:

What is your dream project?

Date & time:
Duration:

Mood/energy:

Goals/plan:

Notes & comments:

"Life isn't about finding yourself. Life is about creating yourself."
~ George Bernard Shaw

Date & time:
Duration:

Mood/energy:

Goals/plan:

Notes & comments:

Date & time:
Duration:

Mood/energy:

Goals/plan:

Notes & comments:

"Success is the child of drudgery and perseverance. It cannot be coaxed or bribed; pay the price and it is yours." ~ Orison Swett Marden

Date & time:
Duration:

Mood/energy:

Goals/plan:

Notes & comments:

"Never limit yourself because of others' limited imagination;
never limit others because of your own limited imagination." ~ Mae Jemison

Date & time:
Duration:

Mood/energy:

Goals/plan:

+

−

Notes & comments:

Date & time:
Duration:

Mood/energy:

Goals/plan:

Notes & comments:

"What you do best, should be practiced least.
Practice is for problems." (author unknown)

Date & time:
Duration:

Mood/energy:

Goals/plan:

Notes & comments:

"Doing the best at this moment puts you in the best place
for the next moment." ~ Oprah Winfrey

What is your greatest fear about becoming successful?

Date & time:
Duration:

Mood/energy:

Goals/plan:

Notes & comments:

"Motivation is what gets you started. Habit is what keeps you going." ~ Jim Ryun

Date & time:
Duration:

Mood/energy:

Goals/plan:

Notes & comments:

"Your attitude, not your aptitude, will determine your altitude." ~ Zig Ziglar

Date & time:
Duration:

Mood/energy:

Goals/plan:

+

−

Notes & comments:

"You will become what you practice." ~ Susan Whykes

Date & time:
Duration:

Mood/energy:

Goals/plan:

Notes & comments:

"Action is the foundational key to all success." ~ Pablo Picasso

Date & time:
Duration:

Mood/energy:

Goals/plan:

Notes & comments:

"I find that the harder I work, the more luck I seem to have." ~ Thomas Jefferson

Date & time:
Duration:

Mood/energy:

Goals/plan:

Notes & comments:

*"If I had eight hours to chop down a tree,
I'd spend six hours sharpening my ax." ~ Abraham Lincoln*

Date & time:
Duration:

Mood/energy:

Goals/plan:

Notes & comments:

"An ounce of practice is generally worth more than a ton of theory."
~ Ernst F. Schumacher

Below, identify any techniques, skills, etc. that you didn't possess (or have a handle on) three months ago, having been gained recently thanks to focused practice and "putting in the time."

Date & time:
Duration:

Mood/energy:

Goals/plan:

Notes & comments:

*"You don't have to see the whole staircase,
just take the first step." ~ Martin Luther King, Jr.*

Date & time:
Duration:

Mood/energy:

Goals/plan:

Notes & comments:

Monthly graphs:

The following three pages feature graphs for tracking the hours you accumulate during approximately three months' worth of practice sessions.

Darken dots on the grid, representing how many hours (on the left) you practiced each day (across the bottom). Later, connect those dots from left to right, creating a jagged line that will be a visual outline of your practice habits. Here's a sample of what it will begin to look like.

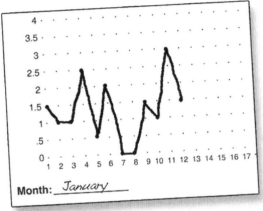

(this awesome graph idea was borrowed from Gerald Klickstein's equally awesome book, "The Musician's Way")

No cheating here; be honest with yourself. At the end of each week and month, take a look at your most recent results. Are you consistently getting a few hours in on a daily basis? Or do you go several days at a time without any practice, followed by a long day trying to make up for it? Is there room here for improvement?

After the graphs, you'll find a "graph math" page, where you can add up the total hours you've practiced during the three months in this book. Also write that number in the space provided for it on the book's back cover.

← Hours practiced

6 ·
5.5 ·
5 ·
4.5 ·
4 ·
3.5 ·
3 ·
2.5 ·
2 ·
1.5 ·
1 ·
.5 ·
0 ·

1 2 3 4 5 6 7 8 9 10 11 12 13 14 15 16 17 18 19 20 21 22 23 24 25 26 27 28 29 30 31

Month: _____   Total hours: ____

←— Days of the Month

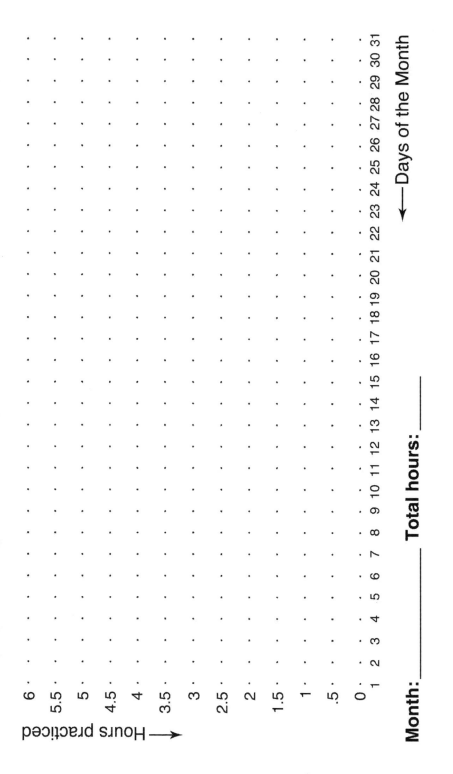

Hours practiced →

6 ·
5.5 ·
5 ·
4.5 ·
4 ·
3.5 ·
3 ·
2.5 ·
2 ·
1.5 ·
1 ·
.5 ·
0
1 2 3 4 5 6 7 8 9 10 11 12 13 14 15 16 17 18 19 20 21 22 23 24 25 26 27 28 29 30 31

——Days of the Month ↓

Month: _____   **Total hours:** _____

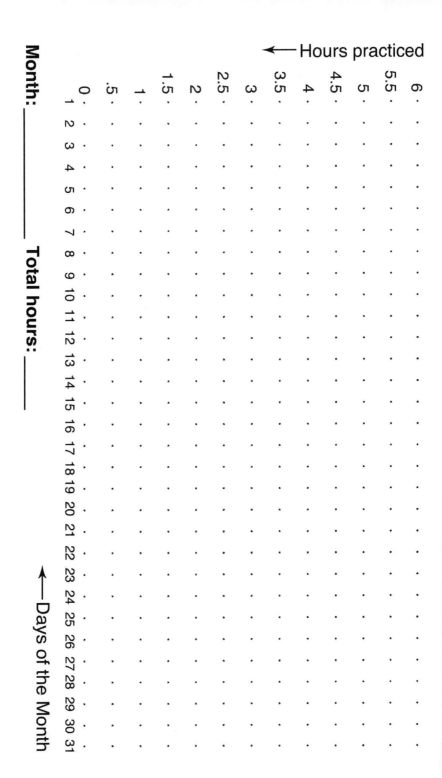

← Hours practiced

6
5.5
5
4.5
4
3.5
3
2.5
2
1.5
1
.5
0

1 2 3 4 5 6 7 8 9 10 11 12 13 14 15 16 17 18 19 20 21 22 23 24 25 26 27 28 29 30 31

Month: _____ Total hours: _____

←— Days of the Month

Graph math:

Month: _____ # of hours: _____

Month: _____ # of hours: _____

Month: _____ # of hours: _____

↑

add up all three of
these numbers

. . . and . . .

write them here

↓

Total hours practiced in this book:

(also write this in the
space provided for it
on the back cover)

Resources:

For more on the 10,000-hour principle and other similar concepts, it's recommended to check out the following books.

• "Outliers" by Malcolm Gladwell

• "Mastery" by Robert Greene

• "The Musician's Way" by Gerald Klickstein
  (where the monthly graph idea comes from)

• "The Gold Mine Effect" by Rasmus Ankersen

As you continue the journey toward reaching your own 10,000 hours, you can find additional practice logs on **Amazon.com**, as well as at **PowersPercussion.com**

Thanks for using this one and keep logging those hours!

72470100R00069

Made in the USA
San Bernardino, CA
25 March 2018